Genre Rea...

 Essential ...
What trad... do you know about?

The Quilt

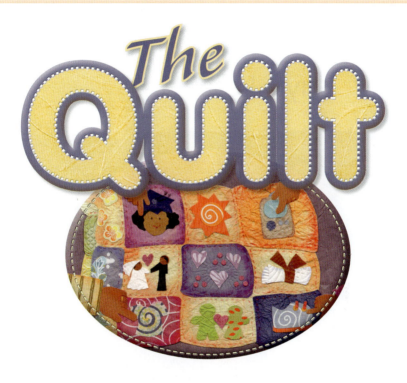

by Sarah Hughes
illustrated by Jill Dubin

PAIRED READ Making a Quilt Square 13

"Leah, come see the family quilt," says Mom. "Your great-grandma started it long ago.

"It's from before I was born," says Leah.

"That's right," says Mom. "Times were difficult back then. Nobody had a job. I heard that great-grandma made this quilt with cloth scraps."

"The front of each square tells a story," says Grandma. "This was our first TV."

"It looks funny," Leah says.

STOP AND CHECK

What is Leah looking at?

"What should we put on our family's square?" asks Mom.

"How about a picture of us planting our spruce tree?" says Leah.

"Great idea!" says Dad.

"Let's use this picture," says Leah.

"I'll have to shrink it to fit," says Mom.

"I'll find some cloth for our square tomorrow," says Mom. "It's getting late."

"Aww," says Leah.

STOP AND CHECK

What will go on the new quilt square?

The next morning, Leah can't wait to begin.

"I'll thread the needle and sew the square," says Grandma.

"May I help?" asks Leah.

"Of course," Grandma says.

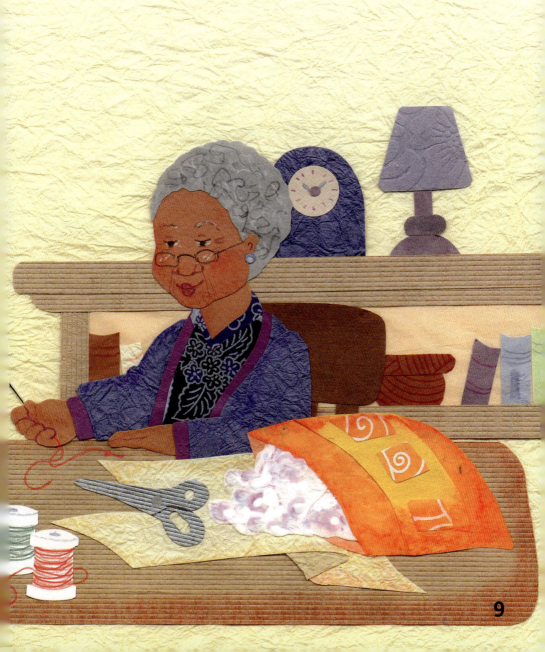

"Leah, can you push the stuffing inside the square?" Grandma asks.

"Yes!" says Leah.

"Now I'll sew it closed," explains Grandma.

STOP AND CHECK

How does Leah help?

"We'll keep the quilt for a year," says Mom.

"Next, it goes to your cousins in Africa," says Dad.

"I wish we could make a quilt every day!" says Leah.

Retell

Use the chart to help you retell *The Quilt*.

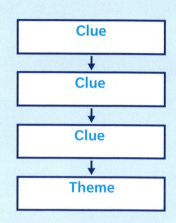

Text Evidence

1. What is the theme of this story? **Theme**

2. Look at page 11. How will the tradition continue? **Theme**

3. How do you know that *The Quilt* is realistic fiction? **Genre**

Genre How-to

Compare Texts
Compare how quilt squares are made.

Making a Quilt Square

People make quilts for a lot of reasons. Quilts can show a part of history. Quilts can keep us warm. People also make quilts for fun. No matter the reason, all quilts begin with a square.

How to Make a Quilt Square

1. Cut two squares of cloth the same size.
2. Sew three sides of the squares together inside out. Have an adult help you.
3. Turn the cloth right side out.
4. Fill the square with stuffing.
5. Sew the fourth side closed.

 Make Connections
What are some reasons that people make quilts? **Text to Text**

Focus on

Realistic Fiction Realistic fiction is a story that could be true.

What to Look for In *The Quilt,* the characters might be like people you know. They do things that you might do.

Your Turn

Share one of your family's traditions. Draw a picture about it. Write labels.